A BLUE BANNER BIOGRAPHY

Shirley Temple

By John Bankston

P.O. Box 196
Hockessin, Delaware 19707
Visit us on the web: www.mitchelllane.com
Comments? email us: mitchelllane@mitchelllane.com

Mitchell Lane
PUBLISHERS

Printing   2   3   4   5   6   7   8   9

Blue Banner Biographies

Eminem	Sally Field	Jodie Foster
Melissa Gilbert	Rudy Giuliani	Ron Howard
Michael Jackson	Jennifer Lopez	Nelly
Mary-Kate and Ashley Olsen	Daniel Radcliffe	Selena
Shirley Temple	Richie Valens	Rita Williams-Garcia

Library of Congress Cataloging-in-Publication Data
Bankston, John, 1974-
    Shirley Temple / John Bankston
        p. cm. — (A blue banner biography.)
    Includes index.
    Filmography: p.
    Summary: Focuses on the acting career of one of America's best known child stars, Shirley Temple.
    ISBN 1-58415-172-2 (lib. bdg.)
        1. Temple, Shirley, 1928—Juvenile literature. 2. Motion picture actors and actresses—United States—Biography—Juvenile literature. [1. Temple, Shirley, 1928- 2. Actors and actresses. 3. Women—Biography] I. Title. II. Series.
PN2287.T33 B26 2002
791. 43'028'092--dc21
[B]   2002008322

JB
TEMPLE, S.
c. 1

ABOUT THE AUTHOR: Born in Boston, Massachussetts, **John Bankston** began publishing articles in newspapers and magazines while still a teenager. Since then, he has written over two hundred articles, and contributed chapters to books such as *Crimes of Passion,* and *Death Row 2000,* which have been sold in bookstores across the world. He has written numerous biographies for young adults, including *Mandy Moore, Francis Crick and James Watson: Pioneers in DNA Research,* and *Alexander Fleming and the Story of Penicillin* (Mitchell Lane). He has worked in Los Angeles, California as a producer, screenwriter and actor. Currently he is in pre-production on *Dancing at the Edge,* a semi-autobiographical screenplay he hopes to film in Portland, Oregon. Last year he completed his first young adult novel, *18 to Look Younger.* He currently lives in Portland, Oregon.
PHOTO CREDITS: Cover: Shooting Star; p. 4 Shooting Star; p. 17 Paramount Pictures; p. 19 Fox Studios p. 22 20th Century-Fox Studios; p. 24 Hulton/Archive; p. 27 Hulton/Archive; p. 28 Hulton/Archive.
ACKNOWLEDGMENTS: The following story has been thoroughly researched, and to the best of our knowledge, represents a true story. While every possible effort has been made to ensure accuracy, the publisher will not assume liability for damages caused by inaccuracies in the data, and makes no warranty on the accuracy of the information contained herein. This story has not been authorized nor endorsed by Shirley Temple.

CONTENTS

Shirley Temple was the most popular child motion-picture star of the 1930s. Today, her films continue to be popular with young and old alike.

Discovery

*T*he 1930s were a difficult time for most Americans. Known as the Great Depression, it began after a stock market crash and ended with the threat of another world war. It was a decade filled with incredible poverty, joblessness and struggle. Even the movie business seemed to be failing. Talking pictures, with their emphasis on dark subjects and drama, were not as popular as the silent movies of the twenties. Several major motion picture studios almost went out of business.

Yet by the middle of the decade, movies were popular again. Musicals began entertaining audiences, while comedies took them away from the bleakness of their lives. Millions waited in darkened theaters for the dimpled face of a little girl to light up the screen in stories promising everyone that better times were just around the corner. She saved Fox Studios. Her face decorated cereal boxes. Long before Barbie, she was the model for over a dozen extremely popular dolls. She even had a soft drink named after her.

She did it all before she was ten years old. By the time she was twenty-one, her career in movies would be over. Yet today her films are still popular.

Shirley Temple was a famous child star in the 1930s. She made dozens of popular movies before she was ten years old.

Shirley Jane Temple was born on April 23, 1928, in Santa Monica, California, a beach community near Los Angeles. Her father, George, was a high school dropout who worked hard and managed to become a banker. Her mother, Gertrude, was a talented dancer who'd always wanted a daughter. Gertrude believed that listening to classical music and reading aloud would influence her unborn child. As soon as Shirley was born, her mother continued her artistic education, singing and dancing for the infant.

Even as a baby, Shirley tried to be the center of attention. With two teenage brothers, George Jr. and Jack, that wasn't always easy. So, when Shirley was three, her mother decided dance lessons would be a good place for Shirley to put some of that energy. The Ethel Meglin Dance Studio was neither the best known nor the most respected. It was, however, the cheapest, and Ethel Meglin promised to teach Shirley the basics of dance. As an added bonus, her studio was regularly visited by people from Hollywood, ten miles away. They were always on the lookout for new talent. Gertrude knew about child star Baby Peggy—the papers said she'd earned over a million dollars. Maybe her daughter could have a similar future.

Shirley was lucky. Where many of the other youngsters struggled, she was blessed with coordination and natural rhythm: she kept her balance during difficult routines and followed the music's beat. She advanced quickly.

Before she'd had ten months of lessons, her skills were noticed.

It was the day before Thanksgiving, and because of holiday plans Shirley took an earlier class than usual. In a rush to leave that morning, her mother hadn't curled Shirley's hair, and she'd dressed her in casual clothes.

Shirley was a talented dancer. She was blessed with coordination and natural rhythm.

After class the two were rushing out when the teacher called after Gertrude. Did she know about the audition?

Despite their plans, the pair changed their schedule. Almost before she knew it, Shirley was standing in a room with two hundred other kids. The parents were taken away, but, as the story is told in Shirley's autobiography, *Child Star*, Gertrude later learned what hap-

Shirley was a natural actress who was able to follow directions from a very young age. She loved to dance and sing.

pened. Writing to a friend, she said, "Little old Shirley walks in through the crowd holding on to another little girl's hand with her little cap over one ear and her elf skin play shoes on and evidently knocked them for a loop. When the children came out, Shirley said that they had talked to her, asked her her name and how old she was."

Less than a week later the little girl was at Universal Studios. Sure she'd been a charmer at her audition, but how would she behave with the hot studio lights beaming down on her? Could she perform with a camera pointed straight at her, a boom mike overhead, crew members on every side? Would she listen to the director? Could she remember her lines?

There was only one way to find out: the screen test. Three-year-old Shirley was given a scene to play and told what to do. As her mother later recalled, "She was crazy about the whole performance, not a bit frightened, did everything they told her to do."

Three-year-old Shirley was given a scene to play and told what to do. "She was crazy about the whole perform-ance..."

Shirley Temple was a natural. A few days later Gertrude got the phone call. Shirley was hired.

Baby Star

G oing to the movies in the 1930s was a different experience than it is today. A ticket, which cost less than a dollar, purchased admission to a single-screen theater. These theaters with high, ornate ceilings and plush seats were a world away from twenty-first-century multiplexes. Once inside, audiences were usually treated to a newsreel, a cartoon, a mini-movie called a short, and two features. Shorts were a chance for actors to get their start and ranged from comedies like *The Little Rascals* and *The Dead End Kids* to serials, dramatic films that ran over the course of several weeks.

Shirley Temple was hired to be in the *Baby Burlesk* series of shorts. Gertrude and George signed their daughter's contract, which was for two years and twenty-six of the mini-movies. She would earn fifty dollars a week—but only when they filmed. She wouldn't get paid for rehearsals. Gertrude was given five dollars a week for "maternal services."

The *Baby Burlesk* comedies were based on popular movies and featured young kids mimicking grown-ups. The characters were an odd combination of innocence and worldliness. On the one hand, part of the young actor's wardrobe featured diapers fastened by a pin the size of her arm—fairly embarrassing for a little girl who'd outgrown such clothing. Yet since three-year-old Shirley's characters were based on parts first played by adult actresses, she pretended to flirt and was often dressed in off-the-shoulder tops.

It was pretty confusing.

Each *Baby Burlesk* mini-movie was filmed in two days. Like most shorts, these films used directors who were either very young and starting out, or old and washed up. The sets were cheaply built. And the scripts read like they'd been thought up the day before shooting.

Gertrude knew Shirley's talent was bigger than the shorts. She just needed the right people to notice. Gertrude secured the services of an agent, someone who would find Shirley acting jobs in exchange for 10 percent of her earnings. Unfortunately the agent wasn't very good, so Gertrude also took Shirley to auditions on her own.

Shirley was first hired to be in the Baby Burlesk series for fifty dollars a week.

At every audition, Shirley reveals in her autobiography, she would confidently walk up to the director and say, "I'm Shirley Temple. I take good direction. If you want me, please tell me what time and what to wear."

It was a tough offer to refuse.

Almost every movie star gets his or her start playing small roles. Shirley Temple's career was no different. In the beginning she was little more than an extra, a small child held or read a bedtime story in movies like *Niagara Falls* and *To the Last Man*. The parts she played away from *Baby Burlesk* did little more than show she could keep quiet on a set—a pretty big deal for a kid barely four.

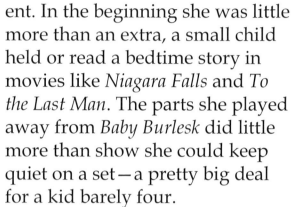

In the beginning, Shirley was little more than an extra, a small child held or read a bedtime story.

In 1933 Gertrude learned about a movie featuring a little girl used to cover a gambling debt: a marker. The role of Marthy Jane in *Little Miss Marker* seemed perfect for Shirley.

The director took one look at the eager girl with fifty-two curls and . . . wasn't interested. Shirley was disappointed, but even at four, she was already learning a basic fact about the movie business. Rejection is as much a part of it as the cameras and lighting equipment.

Besides, there would be other chances.

Star!

*S*hirley Temple's next big break arrived just in time. The company producing *Baby Burlesk* for Universal shut down production. The owners were broke, a common problem in the early 1930s. It's a myth that during the Depression movies were hugely popular. In the period's early years audiences stayed away, saving what little money they had listening to the radio for free at home. At the theater it seemed like a new drama was playing every week — the last thing people needed was to be reminded about how difficult life was.

By 1932 weekly movie attendance dropped drastically. In one ten-month period, attendance fell from 90 million to 60 million. Warner Brothers lost nearly eight million dollars that year, and RKO and Universal were nearly out of money. Fox Studios was also in trouble. *Deep* trouble.

In 1933 the Thanksgiving holiday once again lived up to its name for the Temple family. Shirley and her mother had just left a theater showing *Frolics of Youth*, a short in which Shirley had starred. Beneath the theater's marquee, Shirley was doing a little dance when a man approached her. Where was her mother? he asked. Pointing behind her, Shirley continued to dance.

Shirley's big break came when she had a small part in Stand Up and Cheer!

The man's name was Jay Gorney. He was a songwriter just hired by Fox. He'd seen the short and knew Shirley was perfect for the movie he was working on, *Stand Up and Cheer!* Although the role had already been cast, Jay knew she'd be better. He convinced the film's producer to audition Shirley. This time there was no rejection.

Although Shirley's part was small, Fox executive Winfield Sheehan observed her work and realized she was something special. The camera loved her. He wasn't taking any chances and put her under contract.

On December 21, 1933, Shirley's parents signed a seven-year contract with Fox Studios. Shirley Temple's new wages—$150 a week—were more than her father earned. Even Gertrude got a raise—to $25 a week.

Despite the opportunity, Shirley's parents knew their daughter was signing with a troubled studio. Beginning in the late 1920s the studio lost an enormous amount of money. By 1932, Fox Studios owed millions of dollars. They needed a star to break their losing streak. No one expected the little girl to be Fox's savior.

She was just a contract player, another in the hundreds of actors signed to Fox every year. In January of 1934, Shirley writes, Sheehan did more than announce her employment at the studio when he said, "Four-year-old Shirley Temple has been given a long-term contract." He also changed her age: Shirley was really five. Many actors lie about their age, and the studio decided to make Shirley a year younger. Unfortunately, because Shirley's birth certificate was altered, she didn't discover her real age until her thirteenth birthday.

In the late 1920s, Fox Studios ran into financial trouble. They needed a star to break their losing streak.

The contract meant Shirley and her parents would have little say in what movies she was in. Unlike today, stars worked for one studio, the studio paid for everything from dance lessons to makeovers, and in return the "contract players" were expected to do whatever the studio wanted them to. For Shirley Temple, like many of the talented stars of her day, this would eventually become a problem.

In the beginning, Shirley's roles at Fox were similar to ones she'd already played—bit parts. In 1934 she was

Spencer Tracy's daughter in *Now I'll Tell*; she also did a walk-on that year in *Change of Heart*. It was *Little Miss Marker*—a job for which she'd been rejected—that would change not only her fortunes, but also the fortunes of Fox Studios. And it wasn't even their movie.

A Paramount film, *Little Miss Marker* was in preproduction, the last period before a movie is made. Gertrude managed to get a copy of the script and learned the lead role was still available. She was able to get a meeting with the movie's director, Alexander Hall. In her second audition, Shirley only had to say a few lines. This time she got the job.

Despite her exclusive contract, she was able to do the movie because Paramount agreed to pay Fox Studios $1,000 a week, an $825 profit for the studio.

Little Miss Marker told the story of a girl left as collateral—something of value to cover a debt. Shirley played the marker, the child abandoned after her father loses a twenty-dollar bet. It was her first starring role in a major motion picture. She had to be tough, she had to be funny, she even had to cry. To get her to do this, the director told Shirley her mom had been kidnapped. It was a dirty trick. Besides, Shirley was a pro. She *knew* how to cry on cue.

Little Miss Marker was an instant hit. At one New York theater alone it earned $100,000 in three weeks. The movie only cost $200,000 to make. The profits went to Paramount, and Fox realized they had a potential superstar under contract. Shirley Temple's days of being a bit player were over.

Unlike many child stars, Shirley's movies were meant for all ages, not just kids. Although she costarred

Shirley is seen here with the cast of "Little Miss Marker":
Dorothy Dell, Charles Bickford, and Adolphe Menjou, along with
two unidentified gentlemen. It was Little Miss Marker *that*
really made Shirley a star and changed the fortunes of Fox.

with some of the best-known actors of the day, including Gary Cooper, Joel McCrea and Carole Lombard, Shirley Temple was the star of her movies. It was her name that appeared above the title.

Making films at Fox was nothing like making shorts. Besides well-known actors, these movies employed the best directors, costumers, and writers. The only thing they had in common with the shorts was how quickly they were filmed. "One take Shirley" did her scenes with few mistakes. Every night instead of a bedtime story, her mother would read from the next day's scenes. By going over her lines the day before, Shirley rarely stumbled during shooting. She hardly ever forgot a word or a dance step.

Shirley's success arrived quickly after her first films were released. The audience responded immediately to the little girl with the sunny attitude and enthusiastic song-and-dance routines. She played characters who were sometimes mischievous, sometimes sweet, but always hopeful.

Shirley's success arrived quickly after her first films were released.

Made for several hundred thousand dollars, movies like *Baby Take a Bow* and *Bright Eyes* earned over one million dollars each. Today *Bright Eyes* is remembered for introducing Shirley's best-known song, "On the Good Ship Lollipop." In 1934 it was known at Fox as the first of many Shirley Temple movies to lead the studio to profitability. By 1935 they were making more money than they were spending—over one million dollars more. Shirley benefited as well. She received a series of raises—eventually she'd earn over $60,000 a movie. She received money from a series of dolls designed after her, and from a variety of other products that bore her name. During the course of her film career, she would earn over three million dollars.

Shirley with actor James Dunn during rehearsals for the film,
Baby Take a Bow, *1934.*

In 1935, with her movies doing so well at the box office, Fox Studios was ready to take a risk with Shirley. They'd pair her with another dancer, an adult as talented as she was.

The man they selected would become a legend. But in the 1930s, his casting caused the first controversy of Shirley's career.

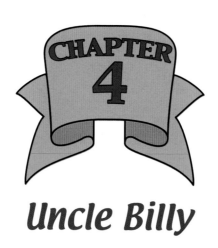

Uncle Billy

*B*ill "Bojangles" Robinson was scarcely older than Shirley Temple when he made his own professional debut. He was eight years old in the 1880s when he began dancing for pennies outside a theater in Richmond, Virginia. As a teen he left the sidewalks for the stage, performing on vaudeville, the loose collection of theaters featuring everything from comedy and magic to dance. As an African American, Bill was forced to perform on the Theater Owners Booking Association's circuit, which handled black performers.

As an innovator, Bill developed a tap routine known as the buck dance. It became his signature: a flat-footed series of steps where his upper body was nearly immobile and his body weight pounded the stage. It was a precision routine, and one that became popular enough that he was able to "graduate" to the

Keith-Albee circuit, which handled mainly white performers. Here again he faced prejudice, as the theaters booked only one black act a performance.

Although it would take television's popularity in the 1950s to completely kill vaudeville, by the time of the Great Depression, it was already dying. Bill Robinson found getting work harder and harder — eventually he found refuge on Broadway, appearing in *Black Birds on Broadway* and *Brown Buddies* at the Paramount Theater in New York City. It was there he was seen by William Sheehan in 1935. Sheehan knew he'd found Shirley's costar. Robinson realized his best opportunities were in the bright lights of Hollywood. He'd already done two small bits in movies, so when Sheehan offered him a contract, Robinson was eager to sign.

As a talented dancer, the man known as Bojangles was the perfect costar for Shirley Temple. Still, the choice was controversial. The southern United States was segregated: African Americans attended separate schools, could only view movies from balconies and weren't even allowed to drink from the same water fountains as whites. Racial prejudice wasn't limited to the South, as Bill Robinson had learned in his vaudeville days.

> *As a talented dancer, the man known as Bojangles was the perfect costar for Shirley Temple.*

Shirley appeared in several films in the 1930s with dancer Bill 'Bojangles' Robinson. This photograph was a promotion for their movie The Little Colonel.

In 1998 Shirley told *Jet Magazine* that the man she called Uncle Billy would eventually become her "favorite star" of them all. The two hit it off immediately, which was a good thing. In the first of the four movies the pair did together, *The Little Colonel,* a complicated staircase dance was the featured number. Bill spent many hours teaching Shirley the routine.

In order to hedge their bets, Fox had crafted a story in which the setting was a Civil War–era Southern plantation. The studio bosses hoped this would appease the Southern audience. The studio even cut out of the movie the few moments during which Shirley's and Bill's hands touched.

The Little Colonel was the first of four movies that Shirley and Bill Robinson starred in together.

The movie was a huge success, earning good reviews—the *New York Film Review* called it "a nostalgic flight in times of stern realities." While the servant role of Bill's character seems tragically stereotypical today, in the 1930s it shattered barriers. Shirley Temple and Bill "Bojangles" Robinson were the first interracial dancing couple in movie history.

Shirley's other parts were not as controversial. They were designed as escapism—a way for audiences to forget their troubles for a while and disappear into light entertainment.

In the middle 1930s, Shirley's movies earned more than those of any other star—she was box office champion from 1935 to 1938. In 1935, Shirley Temple was invited to attend the Academy

Shirley starred in The Little Princess *based on the classic story* The Secret Garden.

Awards. Sitting with her parents, watching the show, Shirley was stunned to hear her name announced as a winner. She knew what to do. She ran to the stage.

Shirley didn't care much for the presenter, a man who insisted she give him a kiss before he gave her the award. Shirley didn't care much for the prize, either. It was a "special" award—it wasn't in a regular category and the Oscar trophy was half the standard size. Shirley didn't think this was very funny. Just because she was smaller than the grown-ups, it didn't mean she wasn't just as big an actor.

By the late 1930s, Fox was no longer on the brink of ruin. It owed much of this to one little girl. There was just one major drawback to counting on a child to fix an adult business.

Shirley Temple was growing up.

So This is Growing Up

*E*very year, movie theater owners conduct a popularity poll. From 1935 to 1938, four years in a row, Shirley Temple was number one. However, in 1939 she dropped from first to fifth, and teen actor Mickey Rooney replaced her at the top.

There was a reason. Shirley was growing up, but the people at Fox seemed unwilling to let her. Costumers dressed Shirley in skirts meant for a child, while other girls her age wore their hemlines below the knee. The studio wouldn't let her experiment with new hairstyles or otherwise change her image. Worst of all, the stories were repetitive. It seemed like the only role the studio would let Shirley play was a plucky orphan. Shirley was an actress—she wanted to be challenged. In fact, she would have loved to play a darker role, maybe even an unlikable character. In 2000, she told *The Films* of the Golden Age Magazine, "Even [well-known theater actress] Sarah Bernhardt would have had trouble given the kinds of scripts I was offered. I defy anyone to have done better with the kinds of bland roles I was given." She was cast in movies that seemed geared for a young audience, like *Heidi* and *Rebecca of Sunnybrook Farm.* Adults stayed away.

Shirley was originally cast as Dorothy in The Wizard of Oz. But Fox Studio would not loan her out.

When Metro-Goldwyn-Mayer (MGM) asked her to play Dorothy in *The Wizard of Oz*, Fox studio head Darryl F. Zanuck wouldn't loan her out. Instead he cast her in *The Blue Bird,* an expensive flop, while *The Wizard of Oz* went on to become a classic.

By then Shirley was attending the exclusive Westlake School for Girls. It was a new experience for someone who'd been educated by on-set tutors, but after a period of adjustment she made friends and began living as a "normal" girl. Instead of just a few weeks between pictures, her time off stretched to months.

On May 12, 1940, Shirley was released from her contract thirteen months early. In a press release, Fox chairman Joseph M. Schenck said, "I look forward to Shirley someday winning as great popularity as an actress as she has as a child star."

The comment was unnecessarily cruel: Shirley already was an actress! MGM believed she was more than a child star and signed her a few months later. The thirteen-year-old received $2,500 a week; her mother got $1,000 a week.

Unfortunately, Shirley Temple's films as a teenager failed to attract an audience. Some, like *The Bachelor and the Bobby-Soxer,* which costarred Cary Grant, went on to be classics. Others, like *That Hagen Girl,* which featured future United States president Ronald Reagan, were less memorable.

In 1945, at seventeen, Shirley married Air Force Sergeant John Agar. The two had one child, Linda Susan, who was born in 1948. John was an alcoholic and unfaithful; the couple would divorce in 1949. He would

When Shirley was seventeen, she married Air Force Sergeant John Agar, shown here. They had one child, Linda Susan, who was born when Shirley was twenty years old. The Agars divorced in 1949.

go on to a mediocre acting career, and died in 2002 at age eighty-one.

In 1950 Shirley married Charles Black and retired from movies. That year, she also discovered that her father had lost most of her money in bad investments and supporting a lavish lifestyle.

Shirley married Charles Black in 1950. They are seen here in 1953 at the premiere of the film Roman Holiday.

Charles and Shirley would have two children: Lori Alden and Charles Jr. Although she would host two TV programs from 1958 to 1961, by then her interest in show business had faded. Instead she found fulfillment in a career in public service, first with a 1969 appointment by President Richard Nixon as a delegate to the United Nations and later as an ambassador to Ghana in 1974 and to Czechoslovakia in 1989.

In 1972 Shirley was diagnosed with breast cancer. She underwent a mastectomy, an operation in which a cancerous breast is removed. Not only did she recover, but Shirley later spoke openly of her operation, giving courage to many other women who faced the illness.

Later in life, Shirley found fulfillment in a career in public service.

In September 2002, Fox Studios unveiled a bronze statue of Shirley Temple on one of its lots in Hollywood. Sculpted by Nigel BPG, it stands near the Shirley Temple Child Care Center. A plaque on the statue says, "Inspiring children of all ages—Shirley Temple."

Although Shirley Temple has made many accomplishments as an adult, to her legions of fans she is still remembered as the little girl with a sparkling smile and curly hair. She will always be a child star.

CHRONOLOGY

1928 Shirley Jane Temple is born on April 23 in Santa Monica, California
1931 Begins studying at the Ethel Meglin Dance Studio
1931 Earns first acting work in film series titled *Baby Burlesk*
1933 Cast in first major film, *Stand Up and Cheer!*; signs seven-year contract with Fox Studios
1935 Awarded "special Oscar" at the Academy Awards
1936 Box Office Champion—for the next three years her films will earn more than those of any other movie star; enrolls in the Westlake School for Girls
1939 *The Wizard of Oz* premieres with Judy Garland in the lead role, a part for which Shirley was originally cast
1945 Marries John Agar; graduates from Westlake
1948 Linda Susan is born
1949 Divorces John Agar
1950 Retires from making movies; marries Charles Black
1952 Charles Jr. is born
1954 Lori Alden is born
1969 Delegate to the United Nations
1972 Diagnosed with breast cancer; has a mastectomy and recovers
1974 U.S. ambassador to Ghana
1976 U.S. Chief of Protocol
1988 Publishes her autobiography, *Child Star*
1989 U.S. ambassador to Czechoslovakia
1998 Recipient of Kennedy Center Honors
2002 Her statue, cast in bronze by Nigel BPG, is unveiled at Fox Studios during the dedication of their Shirley Temple Child Care Center

SELECTED FILMOGRAPHY

1932	*What's to Do?*	1936	*Dimples*
1932	*War Babies*	1937	*Wee Willie Winkie*
1932	*The Red-Haired Alibi*	1937	*Heidi*
1932	*Kid's Last Stand*	1938	*Rebecca of Sunnybrook Farm*
1932	*Kid "in" Africa*		
1934	*Stand Up and Cheer!*	1938	*Just Around the Corner*
1934	*Change of Heart*	1938	*Little Miss Broadway*
1934	*Little Miss Marker*	1939	*The Little Princess*
1934	*Now I'll Tell*	1942	*Miss Annie Rooney*
1934	*Baby Take a Bow*	1944	*I'll Be Seeing You*
1934	*Bright Eyes*	1945	*Kiss and Tell*
1934	*Managed Money*	1947	*Honeymoon*
1935	*The Little Colonel*	1947	*The Bachelor and the Bobby-Soxer*
1935	*Our Little Girl*		
1935	*The Littlest Rebel*	1947	*That Hagen Girl*
1935	*Curly Top*	1948	*Fort Apache*
1936	*Poor Little Rich Girl*	1949	*Mr. Belvedere Goes to College*
1936	*Captain January*		
1936	*Stowaway*	1949	*Adventure in Baltimore*

FOR FURTHER READING

Books for Young Adults

Blashfield, Jean F. *Shirley Temple Black: Actor and Diplomat* (Ferguson's Career Biography Series). Chicago: Ferguson Publishing, 2001.

Burdick, Loraine. *The Shirley Temple Scrapbook.* Middle Village, N.Y.: Jonathan David Publishers, 2001.

Edwards, Anne. *Shirley Temple: American Princess.* New York: Berkeley Publishing Group, 1989.

On the Web

The Internet Movie Database: www.imdb.com

Shirley Temple Fans: www.shirleytemplefans.com

INDEX